DRAW KAWAII IN 5 SIMPLE STEPS

union
square
kids

NEW YORK

Illustrated by
Jess Bradley

Edited by Frances Evans
Designed by Zoe Bradley
Cover designed by Angie Allison

Kawaii is the Japanese culture of cuteness.
This book will show you how to create an incredible cast
of kawaii-inspired characters in just a few simple steps.

Each project has five step-by-step instructions to follow.
Each step shows the new details to add in black line, and the final
step shows what your fully completed picture will look like.

On the right-hand page there's space for you to draw your own
version. The first part of the picture appears in pale gray
line to get you started. Use a pencil to draw the rest and,
when you are happy, go over it with a pen. Then, why not
color in your finished drawings?

Get ready to enter the cute
and quirky world of kawaii …

TURTLE

CUPCAKE

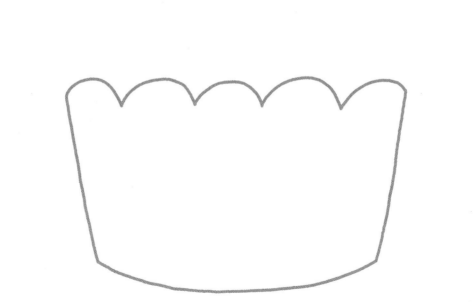

DINOSAUR

TOADSTOOL

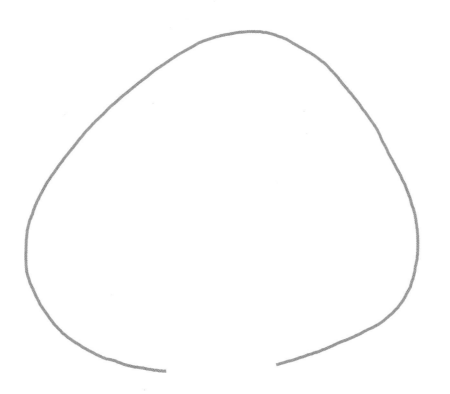

SUSHI

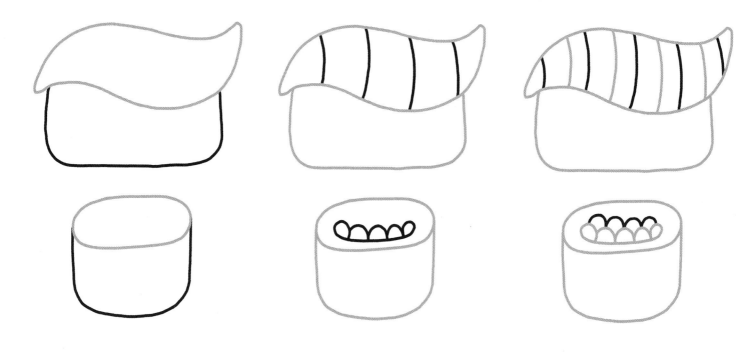

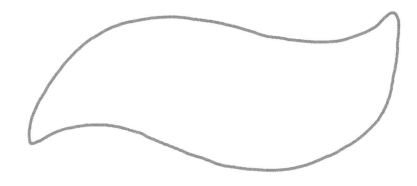

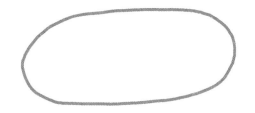

KITTY IN A CUP

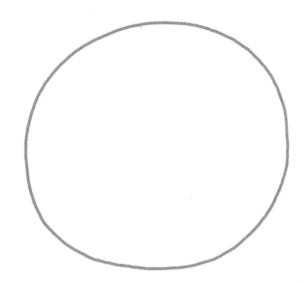

MERMAID

AVOCADO

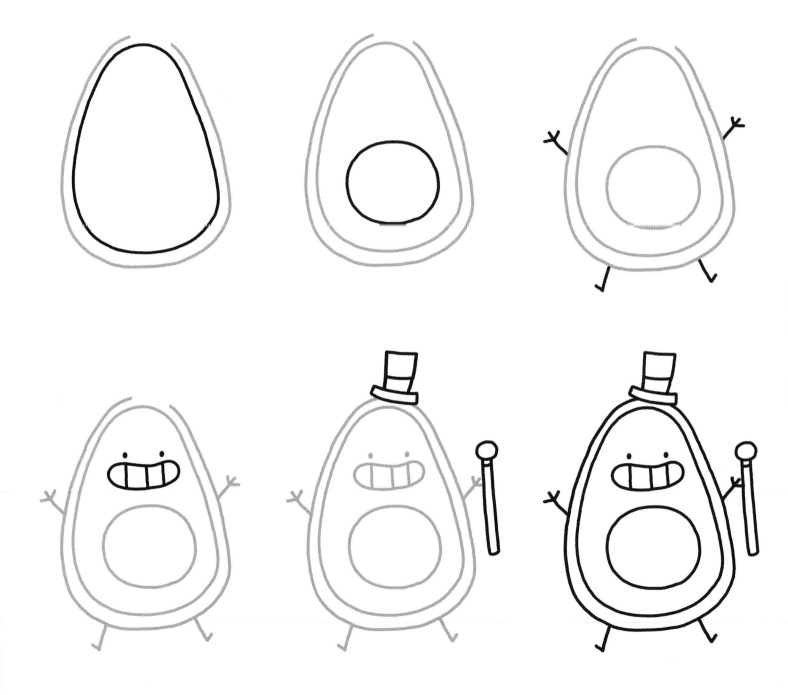

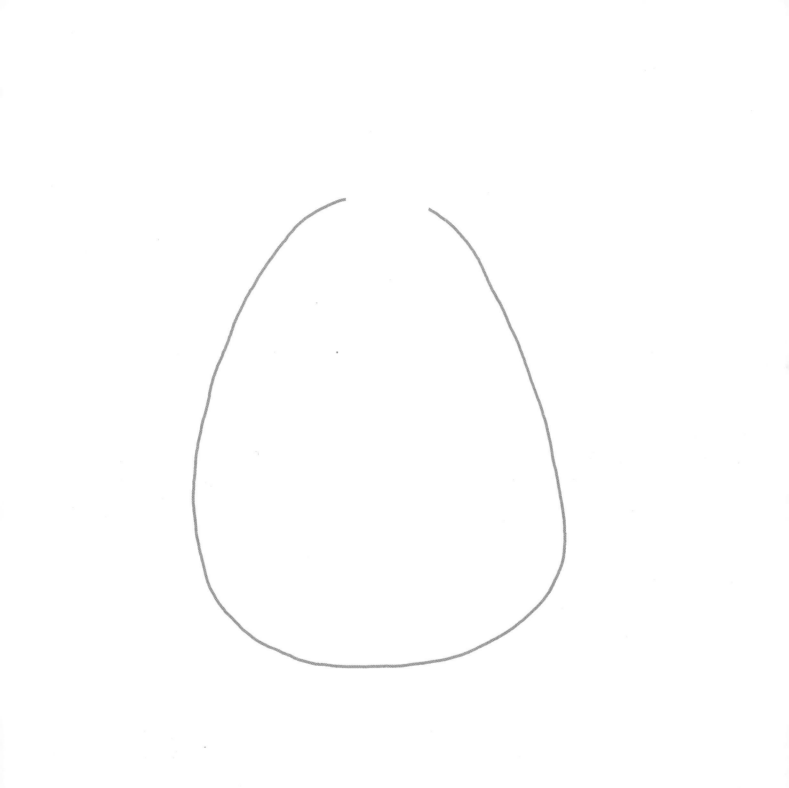

PENGUIN

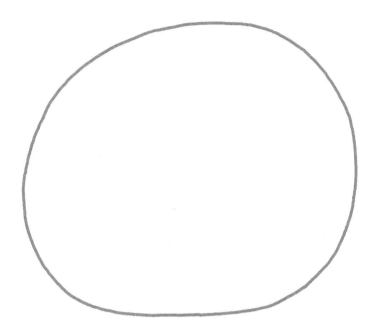

BURGER

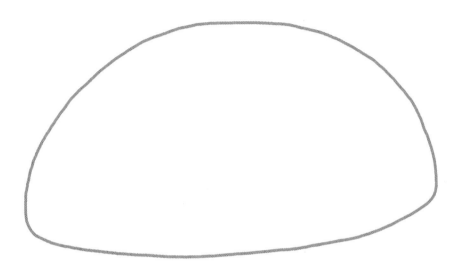

GHOSTS

UNICORN

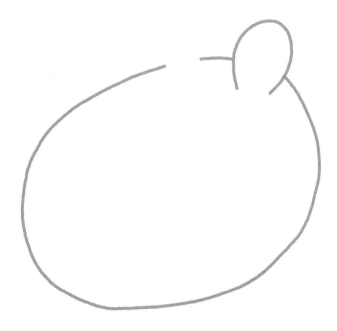

CUP AND SAUCER

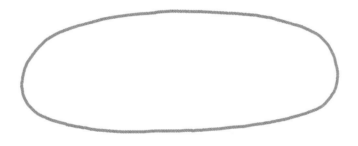

LLAMA

CACTi AND SUCCULENT

PANDA

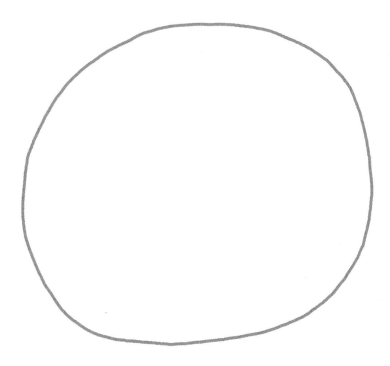

RAINBOW

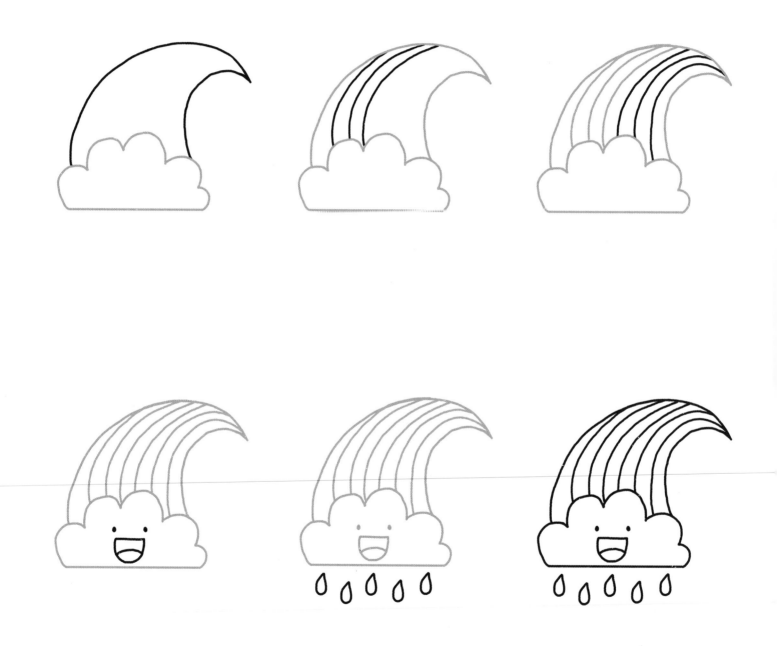

ICE CREAM

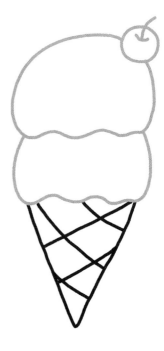

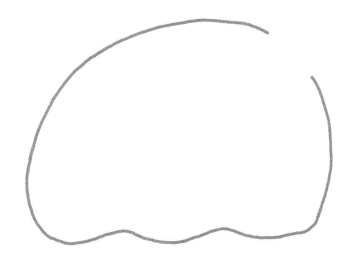

OWL

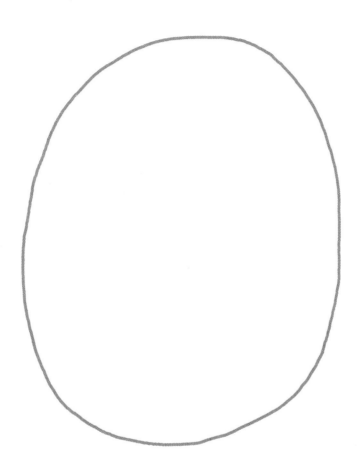

KOALA

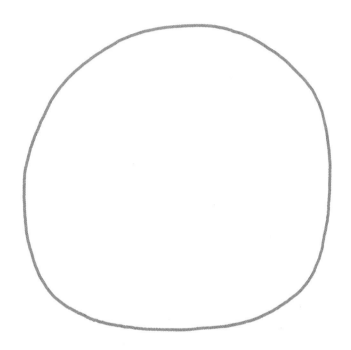

CONTROLLER AND VIDEO GAME

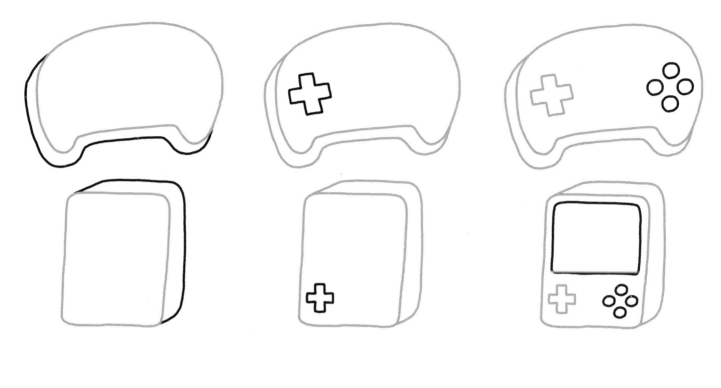

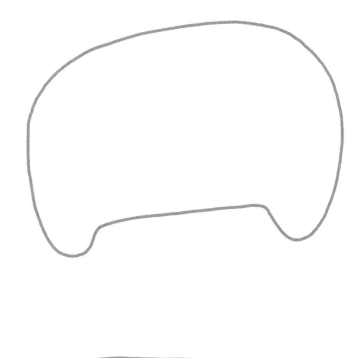

WATERMELON

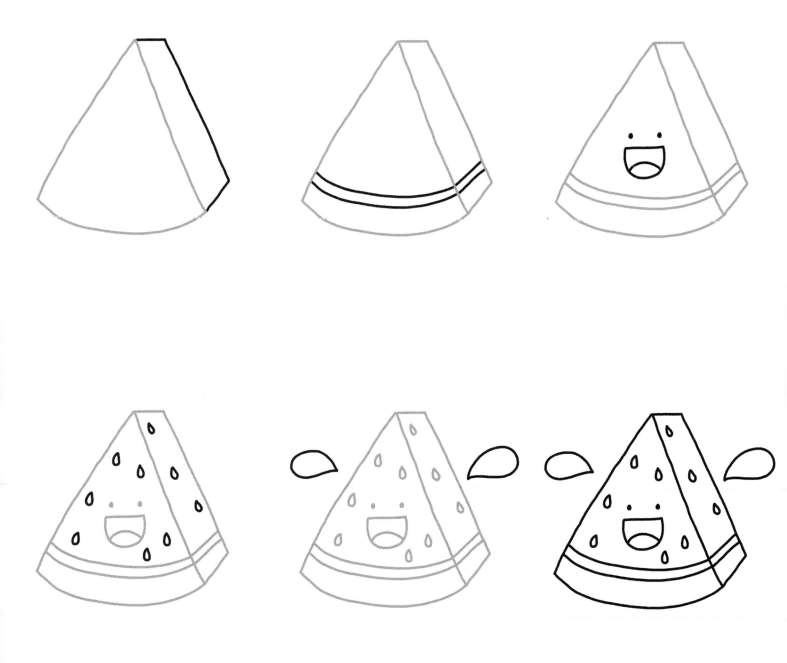

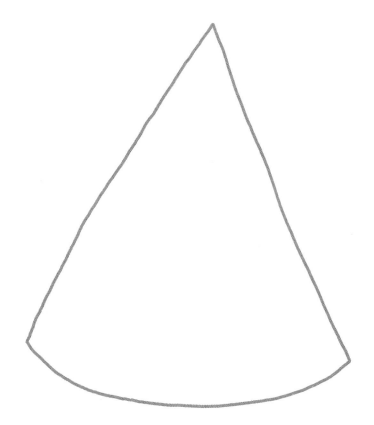

SLOTH

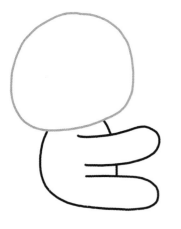

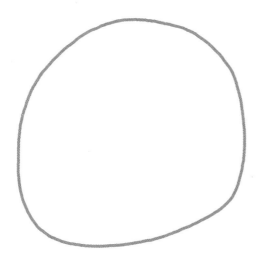

FRUIT BOWL

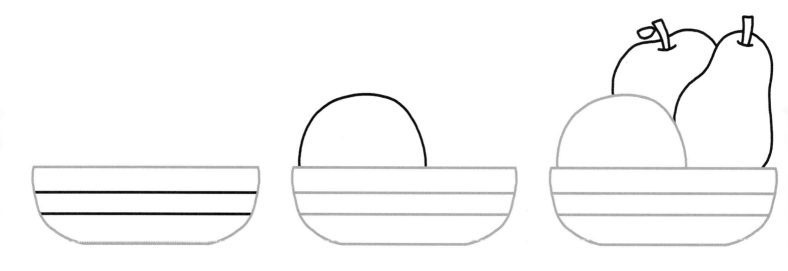

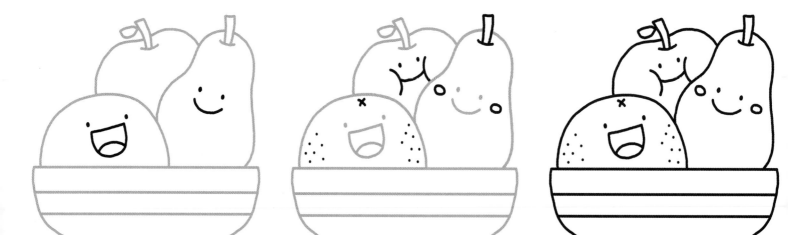

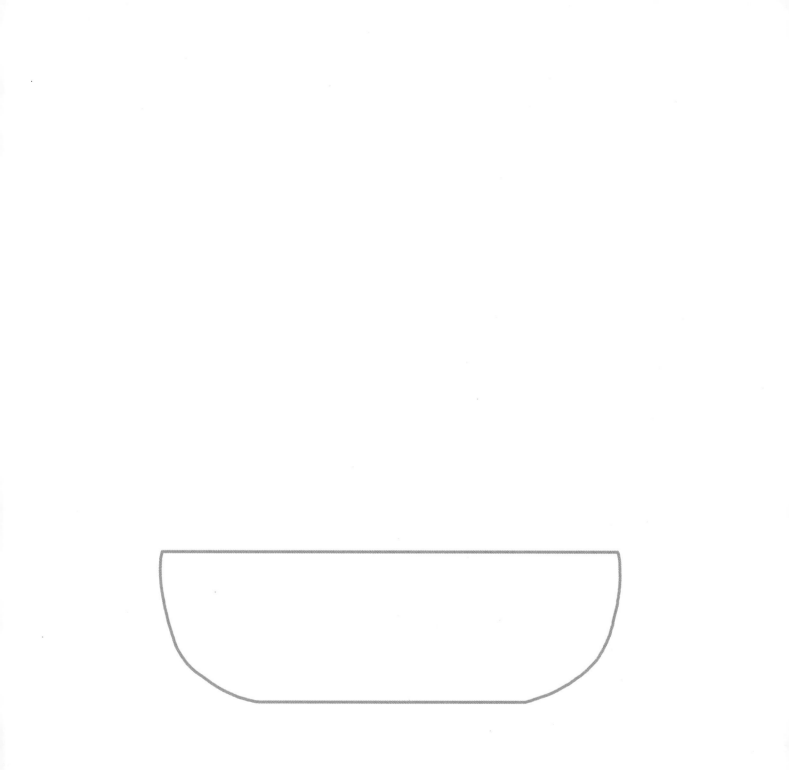

MAGICAL GIRL

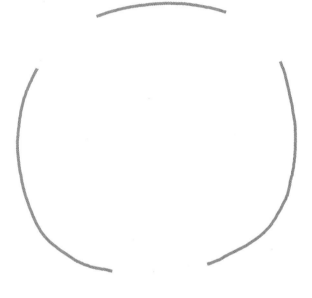

OTTERS

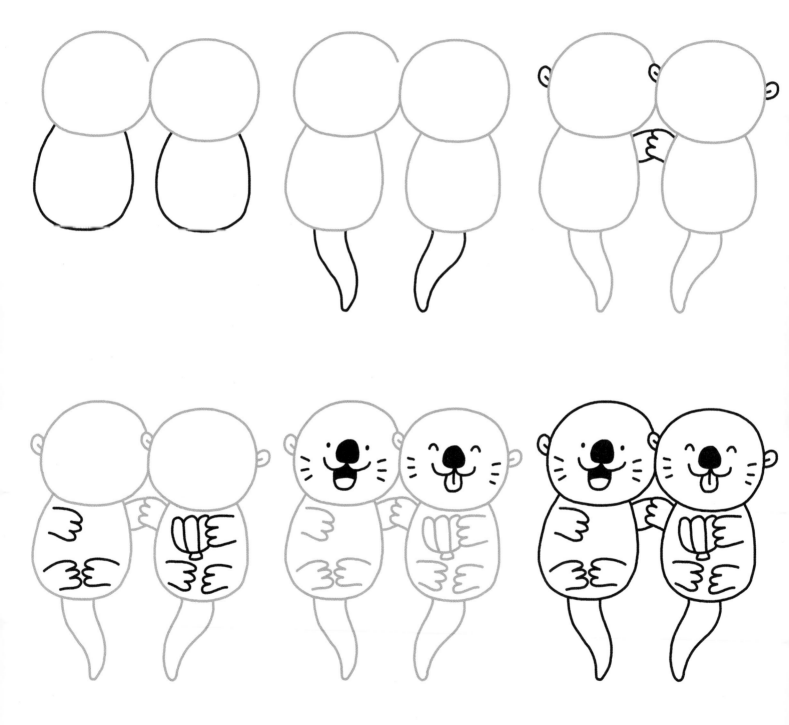

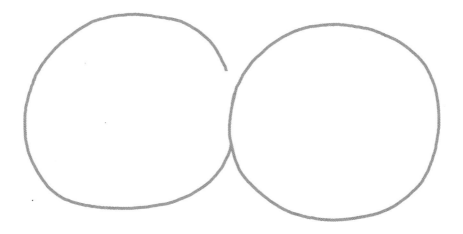

BUBBLE TEA

BEE

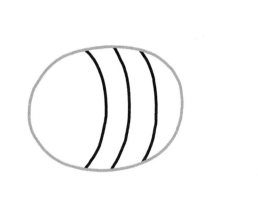

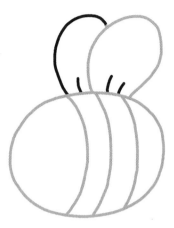

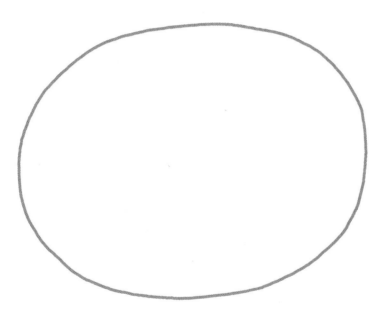

GEMSTONES

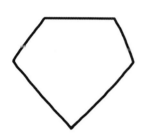  

 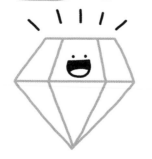 

BOWL OF NOODLES

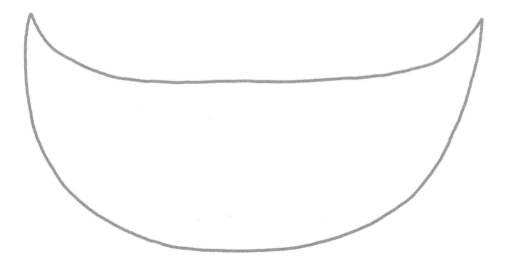

SHIBA INU DOG

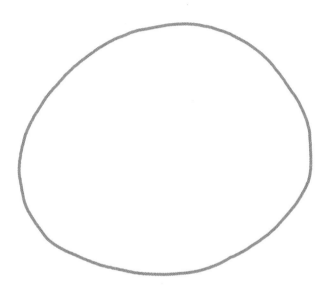

HOT-AIR BALLOON

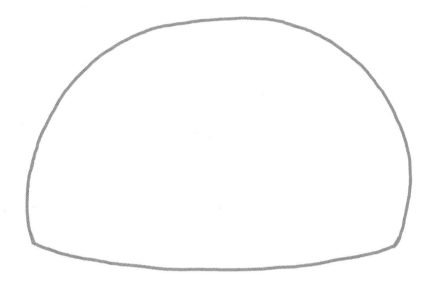

FOX

VEGETABLES

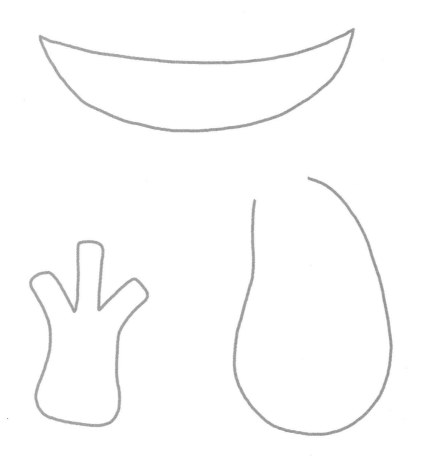

WITCH

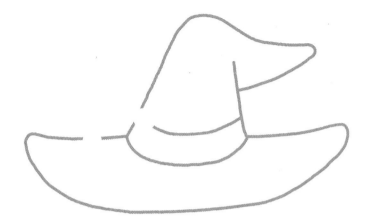

TIGER

DOUGHNUT

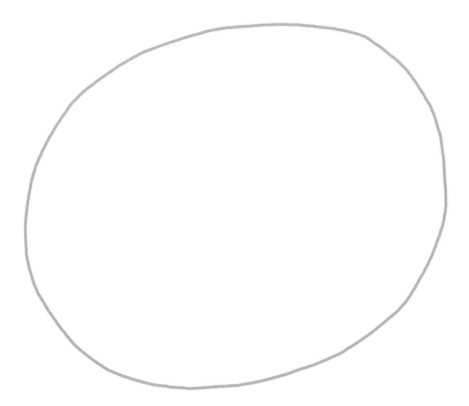

JELLYFISH

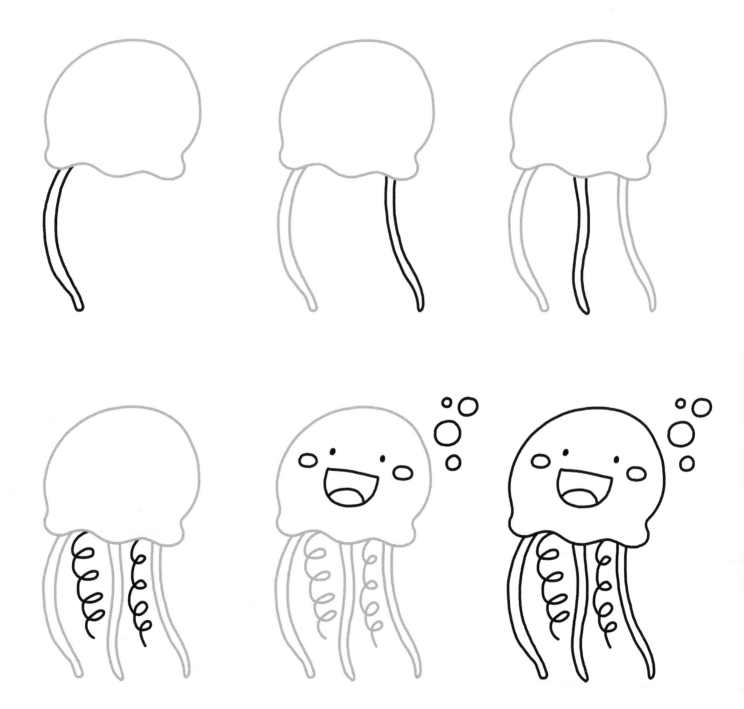